Table
of Contents

Finding Your Bird

For many people, birds are the perfect pet. They are graceful, can sing or talk, are reasonably low maintenance, and are highly intelligent and responsive. It's no wonder that people have prized these animals as pets for thousands of years. If owning a bird is your heart's desire, it's easily obtainable, although it takes a little consideration to get the best match.

Choosing the perfect bird depends as much upon you as it does on the bird. In many ways, it's a harder choice than picking the right cat or dog. After all, all cats belong to one species, as do all dogs. But parrots and parakeets, canaries and finches, cockatoos and cockatiels are different species with different habits, personalities, and needs.

Even small birds like these zebra finches can live a decade or more. Be sure you are willing to care for a bird for her entire life before you purchase one.

It may help to think about why you want a bird. Some species are known for their intelligence or ability to talk. Others sing. Still others are just completely beautiful. In other words, if you want a bird who can hold a conversation, don't get a canary. Some birds are highly social and enjoy the company of other birds and humans. These social birds pine away if not given sufficient attention. Other species have a more independent streak. Dietary needs differ as well. Some birds, like mynahs, have a demanding low-iron diet, others do well on simpler fare, although no bird thrives on just seeds. Large parrots can be very messy, smaller birds are much cleaner. Some birds are better with children than others. We'll look at these qualities in the bird profiles in Chapter 2.

Choosing a bird is not just a purchase or adoption—it's an investment in the future. After all, birds live a long time. I know a couple who received a large (and demanding) parrot as a wedding present. They have now been married 60 years and they still have the bird. She's in their will. Even a small parakeet can live well into her teens. The bird may well outlast you, so if you choose a long-lived bird like a parrot, make arrangements for someone to care for her when you have gone to your reward.

Finding a Reputable Dealer
Once you've decided that you have the time and financial resources for a bird, it's time to find a good source to purchase one from.

Check with your vet, bird rescues, and responsible bird owners to find a reputable seller. Under no circumstances should you purchase a bird from someone who has "set up shop" from the back of a truck or at a flea market. These may be wild-caught, illegally imported, or sick birds. Most of the last legal wild-caught birds came to the US in 1992, but of course, many of those same birds are still around today, having been sold and resold. Wild-caught parrots are usually not as good at talking as domestic-bred ones. Legally imported ones can be identified by the USDA band that encircles one leg. It's best to choose a bird who was bred locally. Hand-raised birds usually make the best pets.

Obtain a health warranty from the seller, since you can't always tell by just looking whether or not a bird is healthy. Still, you can check for the minimum requirements: clear bright eyes, clean shiny feathers, normal-appearing droppings, and a normal gait. A healthy bird is sharp and alert also, neither aggressive nor overly shy. She doesn't seem afraid of you, and it's a plus if she acts as if she likes you.

One of the most troublesome diseases of many species in the parrot family is psittacosis, which can also be transmitted to people. Before you sign a purchase agreement, make sure the bird is tested for the disease (it's not a simple test). To be really thorough, your bird should have a complete physical before you sign any final papers.

Quarantine

 If you already have other birds, quarantine your new pet in a separate room for 35 to 40 days before allowing her to join the crowd. This will help prevent introducing an illness to your other pets. During the quarantine, observe the new bird carefully and take her in for a full veterinary exam.

This would include blood work, throat and vent cultures, and a chlamydia screen. You might also consider some of the viral screens now available for psittacine beak and feather disease (PBFD) and papovavirus.

A good dealer will allow you to take your bird to an avian vet for a proper checkup before the deal is finalized. Don't be afraid to ask the seller questions about your prospective pet. It's important to know how the bird was raised and housed, as well as her diet. If you can't get straight answers, look elsewhere.

The Adoption Option

Because birds, especially parrots, live such long lives, it's frequently possible to adopt one for a reasonable price. Some of these animals simply outlived their owners; others were given up because their owners failed to understand the complexities of their nature or underestimated the care and time a bird requires.

Their long life and great need for attention contribute to African grey parrots being commonly put up for adoption.

Find an Adoptee

To find a reputable bird rescue organization closest to you, visit the Bird Placement Program at www.avi-sci.com/bpp, or call 330-722-1627. Also, take a look at the resources in the back of this book.

Mismanagement is the main reason birds develop a behavioral problem. In the best-case scenario, the bird was simply neglected; lots of sensible attention and care will bring her around. In other cases, however, the bird was actually abused, or at the other end of the scale, coddled, and spoiled rotten.

In some cases, the bird up for adoption has a severe behavioral problem that is beyond the ability of most people to remedy. However, with a great deal of patience, you may be able to rehabilitate even a difficult bird.

In addition, many rescue birds have physical problems due to neglect, poor diet, and ignorance. It's especially important to get these birds checked immediately. If you decide to adopt, expect to pay a fee that will cover some of the rescue organization's expenses.

Finding a Bird (By Accident)

Sometimes people actually find lost or escaped parakeets, parrots, or other exotic birds. Most will die unless returned to captivity, and those who don't can become pests. If you've been lucky enough to find a bird, please call your local humane society, veterinarians, and pet stores to make sure no one has reported losing a beloved pet. If your search turns up negative, you can assume you have a new family member.

Quarantine the bird away from others you may have in a small room (the bathroom is ideal), and spend as much time as possible

Screaming

Many larger hook-billed species are screamers, and there's no getting around that. Many scream at sunrise and sunset, but others at intervals all day long, sometimes for 20 minute bursts. Screaming that goes on for more than that (like for hours) is abnormal and may be sign of sickness or psychological trouble, usually boredom. To reduce screaming in normal parrots, try to change the screaming vocations into more acceptable behavior.

Do not try to eliminate the behavior by screaming back, banging on the cage, or spraying the bird with water. Even if such methods work, they don't solve the condition that is causing the screaming, and the bird may look for alternate ways to express her pain or displeasure including biting and feather picking. Reward quieter behavior with playtime and attention, since the screaming may have started in an attempt to do just that.

socializing her. You can sing or read aloud to her, and if possible hold her as much as possible. When she gets used to you, try doing step-ups and playing peek-a-boo.

Although it may seem easier now to follow your impulse and just buy the first bird who catches your eye, taking the time and trouble to purchase the right bird in the right way will make your coming years together a lot more pleasurable and stress free.

Species Profiles

A rose is a rose is a rose, but a bird can be a parrot, ostrich, or hummingbird. Some species are not suitable for pets, and many are even illegal to keep. In this section, I'll touch upon just a few of the more commonly kept caged birds. I haven't included some really big types like macaws, or some very specialized ones like mynahs or toucans, but you'll get a fairly representative sampling of what's available from this list.

African Grey Parrots

The African grey parrot, *Psittacus erithacus,* is considered by many people to be the best talker of all birds, as well as one of the smartest (rivaled only by blue jays and crows, the geniuses of the

Cost

bird world). The world's most famous African grey is Alex, who can count, distinguish shapes, order people about, and even read.

Appearance: Short-tailed, stocky. They come in various shades of gray, as their name suggests. The tail feathers are reddish or pinkish.
Character: Playful. However, this bird is not as social as many other caged birds and can handle being left alone more than others. African greys tend to do best in a home of mature family members. If stressed, these birds can become feather pluckers. They require lots and lots of toys to keep them interested.
Cost: Expensive.
Diet: Use a specially formulated pelleted food, about 1/3 cup daily.

Perhaps the most intelligent parrot, the African grey needs plenty of toys and interaction with her keeper. This species is also one of the best talkers.

Add another quarter to 1/3 cup fresh fruits and vegetables. A small number of seeds may be given as treats.

Grooming: Normal bathing or misting will keep down the powdery feather dust (to which some people are allergic) characteristic of this species.

Specific Health Problems: African greys are susceptible to the following conditions: bleeding-eye syndrome, cryptosporidiosis/gastroenteritis, feather picking, sarcocystis infection, tapeworms, and tumors.

Housing: Purchase the largest cage you can afford. These are very active birds. These birds require natural or at least full-spectrum light, or they may develop a calcium deficiency due to the lack of vitamin D, which is needed for proper calcium utilization. Perches should vary between 1 and 2 inches in diameter.

Life Span: 25 to 50 years.

Origin: Western equatorial Africa. In the wild, they gather in groups of 10,000 or more, which makes it odd that they don't mind living as the only bird.

Talking Ability: Superb, but don't expect much until they are a year old or so. They begin by mimicking. Wild birds are known for their extraordinary repertoire of mimicked jungle sounds, particularly when the moon is full. According to the Guinness book of World Records, a captured African grey named Prudle had a vocabulary of almost 1000 words. These birds can imitate much more than human speech. They can bark like dogs, churn like washing machines, and buzz like chainsaws.

Canaries

Serinus canarius domesticus, the canary, is a poplar singing bird, with one of the best voices in the business. Canaries were used in coal mines as detectors of toxic gases like methane. If the sensitive birds suddenly died, the miners knew to get out fast. A crude method, but it worked. Various varieties of canary are sold as singers, with the "Rollers," "American," "Timbrado," and "Waterslager" or "Malinois" among the most popular. Canaries are more delicate than most of the parrot species, but they require much less attention.

Canaries have a delightful song and easy care requirements, two factors that have made them popular pet birds.

Appearance: Some canaries are bred more for color than voice, and these are divided into two large groups: yellow or white background and red-factor canaries.

Character: Although these lively birds have been domesticated for a long time, they do not like being handled. Admire them from afar.

Cost: Inexpensive.

Diet: There are some excellent pelleted diets designed for canaries that provide balanced nutrition. If you prefer to feed a seed diet, there are some commercial mixes of 70 percent canary seed and 30 percent rapeseed. You must supplement it with vitamins and minerals. Canaries also enjoy dark green leafy vegetables like spinach or endive, as well as tiny bits of apple or grapes. They do not require grit, although people usually give it to them anyway.

Grooming: Canaries thrive on warm baths twice a week.

Specific Health Problems: Canaries can be susceptible to the following: airsac and tracheal mites, atoxoplasmosis, canary pox, scaly face and scaly leg mite (cnemidocoptes), toxoplasmosis, and trichomonas.

Housing: Cage size should be at least 18 inches square, but a wider space is greatly appreciated by these fliers. Perches should vary between 3/8 and 3/4 of an inch.

Life Span: 10 to 15 years, with some individuals living 25 years.

Origin: The Canary Islands, of course! The domestic canary is a descendant of the wild bird canary, *Serinus canarius canarius,* found there and imported into Spain in the eighteenth century.

Talking Ability: None, but they can sing up a storm. If you want a singer, a canary may be your best choice. Males canaries are superior in this regard, and all canaries sing most if kept single. Yearning, one supposes. Sad but true.

Cockatiels

The cockatiel—formally known as *Nymphicus hollandicus* (even though it is not from Holland)—is a wonderful bird that combines many of the best qualities of parakeets and large parrots with the charm of the songbird thrown in for good measure.

Appearance: Elegant and graceful, 11 to12 inches in length. The natural color of this bird is a powder gray, but domestic birds come in several color mutations, including albino (white with red eyes), lutino (mostly white with a yellow cast), cinnamon (cinnamon-gray), pied (pigmentation lost in blotches over the body), and white-face (white face), among others. The lutinos appear to be subject to certain health problems the others are less prone to, such as fatty liver disease, bald spots, and night frights.

Character: Sweet and sociable. Cockatiels make superb companion birds and are excellent with children. However, it is best to buy a young bird, which can often be identified by a less prominent orange cheek patch than fully mature birds.

Breeders produce a number of different colors of cockatiels along with the normal gray and white. These are active and spirited birds that quickly endear themselves to their keepers.

Cost: Inexpensive.

Diet: A good diet is a half and half mixture of pelleted cockatiel food with cockatiel seed mix. (Don't use a seed mix for other birds, which may contain too much sunflower.) Cockatiels are conservative in their eating habits and aren't crazy about most fruits and veggies, although some like carrots, wheat bread, and shredded greens. Stay away from giving your cockatiel broccoli (it's too high in oxalic acid for them and can result in kidney or calcium metabolism problems). Grit should not be given either. Cockatiels are prone to obesity.

Grooming: This species has special feathers called powder down feathers that can mean trouble for people with allergies, but frequent bathing of the bird will help control it.

Specific Health Problems: Cockatiels are susceptible to the following: *Bordetella avium,* excessive egg laying, internal parasites, protozoal infection, and polyoma virus.

Housing: These fliers need a cage size at least 20 to 24 inches square (big enough so the crest is not crushed and the tail can hang freely), with a least two perches spaced far enough apart to allow some flying. Perches should vary between 5/8 and 1.5 inches. They seem to enjoy natural branch and rope perches. Don't use a sandpaper perch cover for these birds—it's too hard on their feet.

Life Span: 15 to 20 years.

Origin: Australia, where they gather in very large flocks and are actually regarded as agricultural pests. One or two cockatiels is all very well, but in Australia you can end up with 1,000 in your backyard.

Talking Ability: Some can be taught to speak (they have a soft voice), but their main charm is their expert whistling ability.

Sulphur-Crested Cockatoo

The *Cacatua galerita galerita* is a bird of birds with a powerful voice and an over-bearing personality. She requires an owner who is as smart as she is.

Appearance: A very large white bird with a yellow crest on her head.

Character: Playful, curious, bright, demanding. They are also major chewers and can be destructive. Most active in the morning and early afternoon.

Cost: Expensive.

Diet: Pelleted food supplemented with fresh veggies (half and half). These birds tend to get fat, so watch their food intake.

Grooming: Cockatoos can be bathed or misted. Some people dry them off gently with a hand-held hairdryer. Healthy cockatoos should have a fine powder on their beaks.

Specific Health Problems: Cockatoos are susceptible to the following: cloacal prolapse, feather picking, lipomas (fatty tumors), mate aggression, obesity and fatty liver syndrome, picky eating habits, prognathism, sarcocystis, scissors beak, and self-mutilation.

Sulphur-crested cockatoos (and cockatoos in general) require a great deal of attention from their keepers. Be prepared for this before you purchase one

Housing: The cage should be as large as possible. Perches should vary between 1 and 2 inches in diameter. Many cockatoos enjoy an outdoor area in the summer. Cockatoos have incredibly strong beaks, so the cage needs to be especially durable. They are also escape artists and can even pick locks.

Life Span: 40 to 60 years.

Origin: Eastern and northern Australia.

Talking Ability: Not great talkers, but better than most other cockatoos. However, they can be terrible screamers—one of the major reasons they are given up.

Conures

There are many species of these small, comical parrots. For most purposes, the best pet variety is the sun conure, *Aratinga solstitialis*, a golden bird named after the sunset.

Sun conures are beautiful and playful birds that amuse their keepers with their antics. Teaching your conure tricks will help keep him busy and prevent boredom.

Appearance: Slender bird with iridescent colors of orange, blue, yellow and green, just like the sunset. They are about 12 inches long, including the tail. Most other conures are predominantly emerald green, but there is a lot of a variety in this group.

Character: Playful, cuddly, active, good with children. These are climbers. These birds need lots of toys to keep them interested. Wooden toys and loud bells seem especial favorites. They also like to untie things. Annoyingly, some conures make a habit of dropping their food into their water dishes. They find this amusing. You'll either have to clean the dish a lot or else train her to use a water bottle.

Cost: Moderate.

Diet: Conures are pretty easy to feed and like a varied diet that includes nuts, vegetables, fruit, peanut butter, and seeds as well as a commercially available pelleted diet. (They like pellets of different colors and shapes, too.) They even eat a little meat, but I wouldn't recommend turning your conure into a carnivore. It is important to make sure conures get enough vitamin K in their diet (broccoli is a good source).

Grooming: Conures enjoy being sprayed with warm water from a misting bottle. To keep their beaks in order, make sure they have cuttlebones and mineral rocks.

Specific Health Problems: Conures are very healthy as a rule, but are vulnerable to: aspergillosis, conure bleeding syndrome (caused by a deficiency of vitamin K), pacheco's disease, and proventricular dilatation disease.

Housing: Cage at least 20 inches by 20 inches by 36 inches. Perches should vary between 5/8 and 1.5 inches. Conures also benefit from having a play stand of their own.

Quick & Easy Bird Care

Life Span: 15 to 35 years.
Origin: Northeastern coast of South America for the sun conure. Other species are found from Mexico to Argentina.
Talking ability: Low.

Fischer's Lovebird

There are actually nine species of lovebird, but I'll just mention one. Fischer's Lovebird or *Agapornis fischeri* is less common than the peach-faced lovebird, but may make better bets for the pet owner, since they have a gentler disposition. However, they may be subject to more illnesses. This bird is best purchased young; young birds can be recognized by a small dark patch on the upper beak.

Appearance: Bright green body; red face; yellow-orange chest.
Character: Cheerful, energetic, social. These guys want to be the center of attention. And, in case you are asking, yes, Fischer's lovebirds really do show strong pair bonding, as do peach-faced lovebirds.
Cost: Inexpensive.
Diet: Pelleted diet for this size bird supplemented with fruits and vegetables. They do not need grit.
Grooming: Fischer's enjoy bathing at least twice a week, so a birdbath in the cage is desirable. Some also like to be misted.
Specific Health Problems: Lovebirds are susceptible to polyoma virus.
Housing: A cage for a single lovebird should be at least 18 inches square; it should be approximately 24 inches square for a pair. The cage should have at least two perches without sandpaper covers. Perches should vary between 3/8 and 3/4 of an inch.

Contrary to popular belief, Fischer's lovebirds and other lovebirds do not have to be kept in pairs. If you keep only one, be sure to give her plenty of attention.

Life Span: 10 years, occasionally longer.

Origin: Northern Tanzania, where they live in small flocks.

Talking Ability: Limited, but they chatter, chirp, and whistle quite a lot.

Parakeet

Call it a parakeet or a budgie, the *Melopsittacus undulatus* is still the most popular cage bird in the country. "Budgie" is the preferred term in the United Kingdom, while Americans prefer "parakeet," although some reserve the title "budgie" for a show bird. I probably shouldn't tell you this, but the word "budgeriga," from which "budgie" is derived, is an Australian aborigine term that means "good to eat." A budgie is technically not a parakeet, either.

Appearance: Parakeets come in two basic types: the American parakeet and the English budgie. The American variety is about 7 inches long, a lot of that being the tail. The English budgie often reaches a length of 10 inches. The English budgie is more of a "show bird" with a bigger head and chest in proportion to her body; she is less active than the American variety.

Parakeets are available in a multitude of colors and patterns. All make great, lively pets. Parakeets are among the best talkers of the parrot family.

Quick & Easy Bird Care

Parakeets of both sorts come in over 1000 color variations, but the most normal color is a bright green chest and green and black wings. Males look different from females, with the male usually having a blue cere (the band across the top of beak), and the female a pink one. Very traditional of them. (Okay, sometimes the female has a brown cere.)

Character: Parakeets are fairly quiet birds, inexpensive, sociable, and easy to keep. They make a wonderful first bird. They are playful and good with children, too. Parakeets are happiest in pairs or groups, especially if you have a busy schedule. These birds benefit from being allowed to fly around the house at least once a day.

Cost: Inexpensive.

Diet: Wild parakeets live upon greens and ripened seeds. For your captive parakeet, you're safest with a commercial pelleted diet, to which you may add fresh vegetables (broccoli buds, carrots, corn, peas, green beans, leafy veggies), fruit (apples, grapes, pears, cantaloupe), grains (whole wheat bread), and seeds. Add a millet spray once in a while for an extra treat. Parakeets do not need grit, although they will eat it if supplied. Parakeets are prone to obesity.

Grooming: Parakeets are generally quite fond of baths. Some individuals will plop themselves down into a bath; others prefer a gentle mist. Try both methods to see what your parakeet prefers.

Specific Health Problems: The most common diseases of parakeets include: ascarid worms, brown hypertrophy of the cere, capillariasis, feather mites, goiter (common in parakeets fed only seeds), gout, polyoma virus, protozoal infections, red mites, salmonellosis and *E. coli*, scaly face and leg mites (cnemidocoptes), and tumors.

Housing: The bigger the better. Absolute minimum is 18 inches in each dimension. Since parakeets fly horizontally, a cage longer than it is high is ideal. The spacing between the bars or wires should be no wider that 1/2 an inch. Perches should vary between 3/8 and 3/4 of an inch.

Life Span: 15 to18 years.

Origin: Australia.

Talking Ability: Good for the American variety, but many just won't do it, although they may whistle a little tune. Interestingly, parakeets have been reported to have the largest vocabulary of any parrot species, sometimes amounting to hundreds of words. However, they don't speak as clearly as some other species, and tend to use their words as "calls" rather than with meaning, as do African greys.

Society or Bengalese Finches

This unusual bird, *Lonchura domestica*, never existed in the wild at all; it's a purely civilized species. They are more delicate than some of the parrot species, but they require much less attention. The care of other common finches, such as zebra finches, is very similar.

Appearance: Every society finch is a little different, but most are pied, which means they have patches of color. Basic shades include fawn, chocolate, gray, and brown (all mixed with white) and solid white.

Character: A wonderful singing bird for people of all ages. They can be kept together in cages with other birds of their own species or even of birds of another species, as long as they are about the same size. They are usually sold in pairs and should be kept together.

(Select birds who are sitting together on a perch; they are probably bonded.) However, these birds are not fond of being held and are best enjoyed at a distance.

Cost: Inexpensive.

Diet: Society finches do well on a mixed seed diet that includes millet and other small seeds. How-

Although society finches make fine pets in their own right, finch breeders often use them to foster the young of other species.

ever, you will need to supplement with vitamins and minerals. As an alternative, you can also purchase a complete pelleted feed and give seeds for a treat. Society finches enjoy fresh dark leafy veggies (like spinach and endive) as well, and should be offered them.

Grooming: Society finches enjoy old-fashioned warm baths. You can put in a small birdbath for their pleasure and grooming needs.

Specific Health Problems: Society finches are susceptible to coccidiosis, cochlosoma, trichomonas, and yeast infection.

Housing: You need a cage at least 14 inches square for a pair, and at least two perches for these active birds. Perches should vary between three-eighths and three-quarters of an inch. These birds need a cage wide enough to allow short flights.

Life Span: 5 to10 years, with some individuals attaining 20 years.

Talking Ability: None. These are singing birds.

Yellow-Headed Amazon

The Amazon parrots are deservedly popular birds. Several species and subspecies of Amazons exist, with the yellow-headed, *Amazona ochrocephala oratrix*, perhaps the most common. One of the few drawbacks to owning these beautiful and intelligent creatures is that a few cases of unprovoked aggression have been reported. This bird is also known as the double yellow-head Amazon.

Appearance: A fairly stocky green bird with a yellow head in mature birds. Some red on the shoulder and blue tipped wings. They are about 15 to 16 inches long at maturity. Other Amazons may have different markings, but for the most part, they are stocky green birds.

Character: This bird is dying to go to Broadway, or at least Las Vegas—you won't find a better or smarter performer anywhere in the animal kingdom. Mature males, however, can be bossy and even aggressive if not correctly handled. They require plenty of chewing toys. They are bull-headed, as well as yellow-headed—extremely smart and extremely stubborn.

Cost: Moderate to Expensive.

Diet: A pelleted diet supplemented with fresh vegetables and fruit

The yellow-headed is one of the most popular Amazon parrots. They make good pets when properly trained and socialized.

(about one-quarter to one-third cup of commercial feed and the same amount of fresh fruits and veggies). Seeds should be given only a treats. These active birds can become obese if their diet is not closely watched.

Grooming: Regular bathing is essential to this species. Be careful about clipping the wings; clip only the primary flight feathers. Excessive clipping can mean falls for this relatively heavy bird.

Specific Health Problems: feather picking, metal ingestion, obesity and poor eating habits, and toe necrosis.

Housing: As with most birds, the bigger the better: 4 feet wide, 4 feet tall, and 8 feet long suspended about 4 feet above the ground is considered adequate. They love to climb so they need plenty of opportunity to do this within their cages. These guys don't chew as badly as cockatoos, and so they don't need an industrial strength cage (14 gauge wire is fine), but do be sure lock it. They are escape artists.

Life Span: 50 to 60 years.

Origin: Pacific and Gulf coasts Mexico. They live in savannahs and forests, nesting in tree cavities. They live in very large groups in the wild. Other Amazon parrots are found from Mexico to Argentina and on many Caribbean islands.

Talking Ability: Very high, and they can sing perfectly too. I know one who did a fabulous imitation of "Strangers in the Night." On the other hand, they tend to get loud at sunset and dawn, screaming their heads off.

Your Bird's Home

Wwhile in one sense, your bird will be sharing your quarters, she also needs to have a special place to call her own—to be blunt: the birdcage. You can spend anywhere from $30 to $3000 for a cage, depending on size, construction, materials, and bells and whistles (literally and figuratively), but one of the most important considerations is where you will put it.

Location, Location, Location

Your bird should be housed in a sunny, draft-free area where she can be a part of your family's life. The kitchen, while warm, cozy, and usually populated, can be a bad place, because cooking fumes

Buy the biggest cage you can afford. Even small birds like cockatiels, finches, and parakeets need plenty of space for their activities and overall comfort.

can be toxic to birds. Let your bird's personality be your guide. Some animals find too much traffic around their cages very stressful. The living room is usually the best choice for most birds, as it offers companionship without being too overwhelming. In any case, don't exile your society-loving bird to a lonely bedroom.

Most caged birds don't get enough sunshine to benefit from its ultraviolet radiation. These rays facilitate important chemical reactions that enable your bird to make the most of the calcium she is getting in her diet. Window glass doesn't let in any ultraviolet rays, so if possible get your bird outside on warm sunny days. In the winter, a full-spectrum lamp is very handy! Don't put the cage in direct sunlight however, unless the bird has recourse to shade. They can overheat the same way we can. In fact, some birds don't like being placed permanently in front of a window, as they feel they can never relax and must be constantly on guard for predators.

Don't put it directly in front of or below an air-conditioning unit, either, as cold drafts and overheating are equally dangerous. It may help to place one side of the cage against a wall, so a shyer bird can feel more protected. Being completely out in the open makes some birds quite nervous.

The best height for a cage is usually around a human chest height. Cages placed higher than that are difficult to reach. However, never put the cage directly on the floor as that makes birds feel completely defenseless.

Size and Shape

In almost every case, bigger is better. Large birds obviously need lots of space, but even small birds like finches and canaries enjoy flight room. The cage should be big enough (at the very minimum), so your bird can outstretch her wings and flap them without coming into contact with a barrier from several places within the cage. One rule of thumb is that the cage should be at least two or preferably three times the bird's wingspan as well as three times her length, including the tail. Long-tailed birds generally require a tall cage. But in every case, think big. A too-small cage creates extreme stress in birds, which may come out in aggressive behavior, depression, feather picking, and screaming. Who wants that?

Cage Shape

Square and rectangular cages are easiest to care for and least dangerous for the bird. Go with that, and avoid cages with extra corners and other curious shapes.

Construction

While a beautiful antique cage may be appealing, it works better as decoration than housing. Many of them were designed before people were aware of a bird's special needs, and some are downright dangerous, containing traces of zinc or lead. These metals are toxic to birds (and to you as well, if you ate them).

If you have a big bird like a parrot, stick with an all-metal (not wire) cage. These guys are tough and will simply chew through a wooden cage (which are impossible to disinfect, anyway).

Space for Toys

A good cage also should have plenty of places to attach interesting toys and perches for your bird. You should be able to add a good number of toys to the cage without compromising space for the bird to stretch her wings.

Stainless steel is your best choice, as galvanized metal can corrode as you attack it with your cleaning stuff.

Get an easy-to-clean cage—sanitation is much more important than Victorian charm. It should have a grate at the bottom so the droppings can pass through, although young birds may benefit from a temporary paper floor in case they fall. The cage should have a sliding pan at the bottom for easy removal of droppings.

One critical element of the cage is the bar spacing. Quite obviously, you don't want spaces so wide the bird will walk out of the cage. They should be narrow enough, in fact, so that the bird cannot stick her head out through the bars.

The cage doors should open either outwards or down. Don't select a cage with doors that lift up, as they can trap a bird's toes. The door should be big enough to get your hand through and remove the bird if necessary.

Before you purchase a cage, check the cage carefully for sharp edges where your bird could injure herself. You bird will spend a lot of time in her home, and she will explore every millimeter of it. She will also discover and test every weakness, sometimes to her peril. Get a lockable cage; your bird is much smarter than you think.

Perches

Perches are very important to birds. After all, they spend a whole lot of time sitting—or rather standing—on them! So it pays to get some good ones, not just the garden-variety dowels that are unfortunately so common. Dowels are too smooth to exercise your birds feet, and don't really provide enough traction for your bird. Don't use PVC pipe for a perch either; the smoothness of the material doesn't toughen the

Natural branch perches are beneficial to all types of birds, not just parrots. The varying diameter of the branch provides exercise for the bird's feet.

bird's feet and instead leaves them vulnerable to infection. Use natural perches from your backyard or store-bought textured ones instead.

You can use natural wood from the backyard if you are careful not to pick a toxic tree. Natural branches, with their varied diameters, are great for exercising your bird's feet. They also make great chew toys. Willow, fruit trees (like hazelnut), ash, dogwood, and magnolia are considered quite bird friendly. However, be careful not to get a branch that's been soaked in pesticides. Clean and soak the perch in disinfectant and rinse it well before you put it in the cage. Carefully examine the perches to make sure they are free of insect eggs and other disturbing items.

No Sandpaper

Sandpaper perch covers are hard on the bird's feet and harbor bacteria; avoid them.

Put *at least* two perches of different diameters and textures in the cage. Perches of the same texture and diameter cause pressure on the same parts of the foot and can lead to redness, pain, or even infection. One perch should be high up for nighttime sleeping and one near (but obviously not directly over) the food and water. It is important to keep these perches clean after you install them.

You may also want to consider a concrete or cement perch for the top one; this gives the bird a place to trim her beak and nails.

The Play Stand or Bird Gym

Larger birds also benefit from having a play stand where they can hang out, fool around, and interact with you all at the same time. Good ones have many of the same qualities as do good cages: easily cleaned and toughly built. Many are made of polymer and come complete with textured perches. Of course, you can also make your own.

Having a play stand or bird gym will benefit any parrot-type bird, even small ones like Quaker parakeets. They provide an area for your bird to exercise and interact with you.

Quick & Easy Bird Care

Dishes

The best dishes are stainless steel and of a size proper for the bird. They are inexpensive, sturdy, and easy to clean. Wooden or plastic dishes can be destroyed by larger birds, and even ceramic dishes can develop cracks that harbor dangerous bacteria. Clean them every day by wiping them out and soaking them in disinfectant for 15 to 30 minutes. Then wash them out with mild dishwashing soap. Make sure the dishes are completely dry before adding food, as otherwise it can get moldy. Many people sun dry their dishes. You may want to have two sets of dishes, so you can fill up one set while the other is drying.

If you use a water bottle for your bird instead of a dish, clean it with a toothbrush. Check the ball in the bottle to make sure it's operating correctly. You certainly don't want your bird dying of thirst.

Recycle Your Phone Book

Big parrots like nothing more than phone books that they can tear up to their hearts' content. While this may seem destructive, it's preferable to their making obscene phone calls. Put nothing past a parrot. Remove the glossy cover before you give it to your bird, and the pages are perfectly safe.

Toys and Accessories

Birds are intelligent animals who need to keep their minds and beaks busy. Smaller birds may be content with a mirror and bells, but big parrots need chew toys and lots of them to keep out of trouble. There's a huge choice of exciting bird toys out there. This is where you can use your imagination.

Replace or alternate toys every couple of weeks or so to keep your brilliant bird from boring himself to death. However, you don't want to just clutter up the cage with junk. Good toys fulfill a

All birds need toys to provide them with mental stimulation. Choose toys that are appropriate for the size and type of your bird.

purpose: physical, intellectual, or perhaps even spiritual! Birds like a challenge, so look for toys that will make your bird use her mind. For parrots, consider four toys to be the minimum number to have in the cage. Check all toys daily for signs of wear and damage.

Single birds like mirrors, and most enjoy ladders, swings, bells, and chew toys. Swings and closed-linked chain provide exercise. Wood, leather, and hard plastic are suitable materials. Many parrot species also require something hard like cuttlebone or mineral rock to chew on to wear their beaks down. Overgrown beaks make it difficult or impossible for your bird to eat.

Bells

If you select a bell, make sure the bird won't be able to remove the clapper, which can be a choking hazard.

Cage Covers

Cage covers tell the bird it's time to go to sleep. You can buy a commercial one that fits the cage, but any piece of cloth works just

The Ropes

Avoid rope toys, especially for parrots; swallowed fibers can get entangled in their insides. Other birds have been known to strangle themselves with them.

fine. Some people never cover their bird's cage, but it's a good idea to do so if you stay up late. In the wild, birds need 10 to 12 hours of shuteye a day, and they should get about the same amount in the home.

Cage and Perch Care

If you've done a good job in picking the right cage, its care shouldn't be an onerous chore. Birdcages should be cleaned every day; it's an excellent chance to do a mini-health check. You will note during the process if the bird has been eating and eliminating normally, and if there are an unusual number of loose feathers in the cage.

To clean the cage, remove the accessories (and the bird, of course) and wipe down the surfaces. While you're at it, you can check to make sure the cage and toys are in good repair.

Line the pan with butcher paper or newspaper. If you use newspaper, choose black and white only. Colored ink is sometimes toxic. If you have small birds, you can place several layers of newspaper, and just remove the top layers with each cleaning. This saves time. Avoid wood shavings; they can injure the bird's respiratory system.

Once a week, do a more thorough job, and scrub down the cage with disinfectant. You can safely use diluted bleach in a 5 percent solution, or a half-cup or cup of bleach to a gallon of water. Safe commercial products are also available. Avoid pine oil cleaners, which are dangerous to many animals. Let the cleaner remain in contact with the cage material for 10 minutes. Then wash with soap and water, and let everything dry (sun dry if you can).

Careful Cleaning

When cleaning the cage, make sure the bird is not too close by. The fumes from bleach or other cleaners can be dangerous. Avoid scented cleaners since they can damage your bird's respiratory membranes.

Wooden perches should be scrubbed and sanded to get rid of lurking bacteria. It's very important to let the wood dry completely before returning your bird to the cage. It's easier to get a new perch from the backyard, but clean and disinfect it first.

This is a good time also to sweep or vacuum under and around the cage. A hand-held vacuum is excellent for this purpose. Some people make this job easier for themselves by using a cage apron. Of course, that has to be cleaned as well.

Feeding & Nutrition

Good nutrition is one basis for a happy life, and caged birds have been the victims of poor nutrition for much too long. Part of the problem is that until very recently, absolutely no research was done on what caged birds require in the way of nutrition. For a long time people thought it was normal for parakeets to live only three or fours years. Now we know that a poor, fattening, seed-based diet has contributed to their early demise.

The same is true of most other caged birds. And so, while I'll give you the best advice we have currently available for feeding your bird, research is continually ongoing. It's a subject still in its infancy. This is one reason why I recommend supplementing even a "complete" diet with fruit and vegetables, which are the natural foods of birds and which may have nutritional properties not yet incorporated into a formula.

Parrots and Their Kin

Birds in the parrot family can be categorized by the main staple of their diets: herbivores (plant eaters). Some classes of herbivores include granivores (grain or seed eaters), folivores (leaf eaters), and frugivores (fruit eaters).

Feeding Seeds

Birds love seeds, but be cautious. Even birds who depend largely on seeds for living in the wild, like canaries, may not thrive on a seed-only diet in captivity. Part of the reason is that we don't offer the right seeds, the ones they would be eating in their native lands. In addition, seeds are not available all year long in the wild, and birds are forced to change their diets according to the season. (Even in the tropics, the same plants don't produce seeds all year long.)

Cockatoos and other members of the parrot family require a varied diet that includes pellets, nuts, fruits, and vegetables. For these birds, seeds should mainly be used as treats.

We also offer substitute seeds that are lower in nutrition. In addition, wild birds fly hither and yon, looking for food and expending energy to do it. Most caged birds sit around the house and wait for dinner. When it comes, they aren't all that hungry, having not done much work that day. So, they don't eat much. Considering that the seeds they are offered are lower in quality than their natural diet, the bird thus suffers a double whammy: too few seeds and those of poor quality. She may get fat due to lack of exercise, but she's malnourished at the same time.

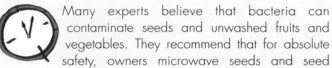

Decontaminate Your Seeds

Many experts believe that bacteria can contaminate seeds and unwashed fruits and vegetables. They recommend that for absolute safety, owners microwave seeds and seed mixtures before feeding them to pet birds. Microwave on high for 5 minutes, stirring once. Wash all fruits and vegetables in tap water that's been allowed to run for three minutes before using on the fruit.

Caged birds also have the luxury of picking out their favorite seeds in a mixed batch. What they choose may be the tastiest seeds, but not necessarily the most nutritious ones. This is like kids picking French fries over broccoli. This kind of picky eating leads to further nutritional deficiencies. You are much better off giving your seed-eating bird a formulated food to which you add fresh fruits and veggies. Even though most seed diets aren't very good, it can be hard to convert a bird who is used to them to a proper diet. They are sort of like teenagers addicted to junk food.

Pelleted Foods

Most formulated foods (pellets, nuggets, and so forth) combine grains, seeds, vegetables, fruits, and proteins, along with supplemental vitamins and minerals. The ingredients are mixed

Find a Supplier

In some cases, pellets are hard to find. Be sure you can get a good supply before switching your bird to them. Try pet stores, feed stores, avian vets, and the Internet to find your source of pellets.

together and then baked. (Some forms are just compressed without cooking.) The resultant product is a uniform (but nutritional) mass from which the bird cannot select her ill-chosen "favorites." Thus the bird is much less liable to develop a nutritional disease. Select a food designed for the species of bird you own. Cockatoos need lots of protein, for example, while many conures need higher levels of fat.

Pelleted foods are not only more nutritious than seeds but are also less messy and more accessible. Often the bird leaves the seeds' hulls on top of the uneaten seeds, thus making it harder and harder for her to access the good stuff. And sometimes, the owner thinks that the seed dish is full, whereas in reality the bird has eaten everything edible. The pelleted form is also safe, since it does not readily spoil. It can be stored for weeks if the humidity is low, but it's safest to keep large amounts refrigerated.

Manufacturers have developed wonderful new formulas that are not only nutritious, but appealing as well. The best ones come in a variety of pellet sizes and colors and textures for added interest for your bird.

However, your parrot doesn't have to subsist totally on pellets. How boring that would be! Instead, the bird's diet can be 50 percent pellets and 50 percent veggies and fruit. While pellets may seem more expensive than seeds, remember that you are not paying for shells with pellets. Another great advantage of pelleted food is that it is much less messy. What a relief not have seed hulls scattered all over your living room.

To switch your bird from a seed-based to a pelleted diet, go slowly. Gradually replace the seed mixture with the pellets until you have reach the 50/50 split. You may have to hand-feed your bird for a short while; select a brightly colored piece to lure her.

Good fruits for psitticines include:

- Apple
- Apricot
- Berries
- Cantaloupe (no rind)
- Cherries
- Grapes
- Grapefruit
- Kiwi
- Mango
- Papaya
- Peaches
- Pears
- Pineapple
- Plums
- Pomegranate
- Tangerine

Good vegetables for most psitticines include dark yellow and leafy green vegetables like:

- Beet and turnip greens
- Bell peppers
- Broccoli
- Carrots (roots and tops)
- Cauliflower
- Collard greens
- Cucumber
- Eggplant
- Green beans
- Kale
- Parsley
- Radicchio
- Squash
- Sweet potatoes
- Swiss chard
- Zucchini

You can feed the vegetables whole or chopped, raw or slightly cooked. Try hanging the vegetables from a clip on the side of the

Many parrots actually enjoy hot peppers, which are rich in vitamin C. Always wash fruits and vegetables thoroughly before feeding them to your bird.

cage. Try some sprouted seeds, too! They have great nutritional value, because the seed transfers its nutrients into a highly digestible, bioavailable form as it begins to grow. You can find information on seed sprouting at health food stores and online.

Be sure to wash all fruits and vegetables carefully before feeding them to your bird, and toss away those that remain uneaten after an hour. Fresh food spoils quickly. Do not allow your bird to eat the pits or stones of fruit.

Feeding Canaries and Finches

In the wild, canaries eat much more than seed. Their diet includes insects, fruits, and leaves. Of course they get lots of sunlight that allows them to make vitamin D. Many pet birds don't get any of this stuff.

Even though they are classified as seed eaters, finches and canaries need some fruits and vegetables in their diet.

Quick & Easy Bird Care

Canaries thrive on a seed mix of 70 percent canary seed (not just millet) and 30 percent rape seed. Use a diet specially formulated for canaries or finches. Be sure to add fresh food every day. Sprouted seeds are excellent for finches and canaries as well.

A good pelleted food is also good for canaries and finches. Pick a kind that is "powdered" or "mashed" and supplement with fruits and vegetables. Wash them carefully and chop in small sizes. Avoid fattening sunflowers seeds, even though canaries love them.

Dietary No-Nos

Some foods should not be fed to birds for various reasons. These include:

- Alcohol
- Apple seeds
- Avocado (guacamole)
- Caffeine
- High-fat and high-salt food (junk food)
- Mushrooms
- Onions
- Persimmons

Grit

Grit is mostly ground up minerals and sand. It comes in two types: soluble grit such as cuttlebone, oystershell, and limestone, and insoluble grit, like silica and sandstone. The soluble sort passes harmlessly through the digestive system and provides a source of calcium. However, precisely because it is soluble, it doesn't help to digest seeds. Insoluble grit does help digest seeds (especially sunflower seeds), by removing the shell and husks, but it can impact in the digestive system.

Finches and canaries need a little bit of grit (just a grain or two) once every couple of months or so, as they do not have the tough beaks to remove the shells well. Since the grit stays in the gizzard for a very long time, you don't need to give much.

Special Birds, Special Diet

Softbilled birds like lories and lorikeets are special. They cannot handle variety in their diet and must receive foods designed especially for them. In the wild they subsist largely on honey, pollen, and nectar and need a mostly liquid diet with chopped-up fruit and vegetables.

Members of the parrot family don't need it, because they can take off the shells themselves with their tough beaks. Grit can even affect them adversely by irritating the digestive system or causing a blockage. One of the problems is that they tend to eat too much of it. If you are not sure whether your bird needs grit, check with your avian vet. If you do buy grit, make sure you get it from a reputable commercial source. Grit can be contaminated by heavy metals and other poisons.

Supplementation

A really good diet should not need supplementation, but if you do add vitamins or minerals, add them in soft food like bread rather than in water. You never know how much the bird is getting if you put it in water.

If you are feeding a correct diet, your bird should not require supplementation. In fact, birds with poor liver or kidneys have been known to die when given supplements of vitamin D_3. This is especially true of blue and gold macaws. And, oversupplementing protein can cause gout.

On the other hand, birds who are deficient in calcium will get soft bones, and calcium deficient females who try to lay eggs may die. Calcium or vitamin D deficiency is most common in cockatiels. Most birds get enough calcium from a calcium block or from cuttlebone.

Amazon parrots, like this blue-fronted Amazon, are prone to obesity. Feeding a diet rich in fruits and vegetables and keeping your bird active will prevent this problem.

Avian Obesity

Like all other domestic animals, most caged birds are overfed and underexercised. To check for obesity in your bird, examine her breast muscle. There is a bone running down the midline called the keel, surrounded by rounded muscle. If there is a clear divide or cleavage, your bird is probably too fat.

When a bird acquires excess fat, it ends up in her liver, and healthy fat replaces normally functioning liver cells. The result is a condition formally knows as hepatic lidosis, which just means liver fat. If your bird is overweight, try to reduce her ounces by eliminating simple carbohydrates from her diet (like fruit) and

Fat Amazons

Amazon parrots seem particularly prone to weight gain from simple carbohydrates in the diet. Owners of these birds must pay particular attention to their birds' weight.

Mealtimes

In the wild, birds dine about half an hour after sunrise and again at sunset. Your caged bird will thrive on this schedule as well.

increase her fiber intake by supplying more leafy greens. If you are feeding your bird nuts, choose almonds and pine nuts over the cheaper but less nutritious and more fattening peanuts.

Water and Other Drinks

Provide fresh clean water every day. Some birds, particularly Amazon parrots, are fond of dunking everything they eat in water as if they were raccoons.

Some owners believe that drinking a lot of water is not natural for many caged birds and suggest substituting apple juice, or other fruit juice. Unfortunately, we don't really have enough information about birds drinking habits to be absolutely positive which is best.

Grooming and Care

Bathing and nail clipping are the two most important grooming chores. Many people also clip the wings of parrot species. A healthy bird takes care of her own feathers, and if your previously well-groomed parakeet starts looking a bit bedraggled, you can bet something more important is going on than absent mindedness.

Your Bird's Feathers

Your bird's feathers are made out of keratin, a protein found in your own hair and nails. Feathers come in different types: contour, flight, down, filoplume, semiplume, and bristle. Each serves a different purpose, but all types develop in a follicle, just as hair does in people.

Birds have two basic different methods of self-grooming: oil or powder. Most birds have an oil secreting gland at the base of the tail, which the bird used to oil her feathers. Others have a special "powder" or "dust" on their feathers (to which some folks are allergic).

Like cats and dogs, birds shed (called molting). In the wild, it's seasonal and rather sudden, but in captivity birds molt rather gradually (and constantly) in response to light change. When the old feather falls out, a new one, covered by a keratin sheath comes in. Your bird (or her partner) will pluck off the keratin sheath, but if she can't reach it, you may have to help. Using your thumb and forefingers like a beak, gently remove the sheath. It also helps to mist your bird during the molting process, as this seems to soften the feathers.

Beak Work

The bird's beak is a wonderful device that has a multitude of uses. It's a weapon, a feeding tool for babies, a grasping tool, a grooming implement, and much more. Birds with hooked beaks are known for the strength of their grasp (or bite). Remember that they can crack a walnut with this thing! Canaries and finches have short straight beaks useful for extracting grubs from the earth (which is what they do in the wild). Check your bird's beak every day, looking for cracks, overgrowth, misalignment, or discoloration of the beak. Beaks in poor condition may benefit from extra calcium supplied in cuttlebones and the like. Chewing toys are also essential to keep the beak in fit condition.

Mineral blocks, cuttlebones, and hard wooden toys will help prevent your bird's beak from overgrowing.

Quick & Easy Bird Care

The greatest problem for caged birds is the "overgrown beak," "scissors," or "parrot beak" (prognathism), in which the underbill extends beyond the upper, a condition most commonly seen in cockatoos. These conditions are characteristic of the parrot species.

Birds trim their own beaks (that's one reason for the concrete perch), but if you notice that the upper and lower beak are improperly aligned ("scissors beak"), your vet may need to help, as this condition doesn't allow the bird to eat properly. Cockatoos and macaws are most frequently affected.

Filing the beak doesn't hurt the bird, but unless you know what you are doing, the job is best left to a professional. Some very tame birds will let you file their beaks with an emery board, but I wouldn't count on it. If the beak is actually cracked, you should act quickly and get her to an avian veterinarian. A cracked beak is liable to hemorrhage.

Nail Trimming

While most birds can bathe themselves, all need help with keeping their nails in order. Nails that are too long will catch and break. They also make it difficult for the bird to perch properly. You know the nails are too long if the bird's toe is lifted off the ground when the feet are on a flat surface. The bird's breeder or a veterinarian can show you the easiest way to do it.

Good Night's Sleep

Most caged birds hail from the tropics where they get between 10 and 12 hours of sleep every night. Your bird should be so lucky. If people in your house are up at all hours, your bird may become sleep deprived. This can lead to behavior problems. Use a cage cover and remove your bird to a quiet room if people are up late.

You can use fingernail clippers for small birds. Look for the vein (quick) inside the nail. If the nails are white, this is easy, not so if they are dark. Trim off tiny bits at a time, while restraining the bird. In some cases, you can even use an emery board, if your bird is tame. Don't feel as if you have to do them all at once. Do one or two a day, as it's less stressful for the bird. Large birds often benefit from having their nails ground with a dremel tool or other rotary grinder.

If you clip too close and the nail bleeds, you can apply a styptic powder or even flour or cornstarch. Alternatively, use a small piece of soap. Squeeze the toe just above the claw (to make a temporary tourniquet). Then, apply the styptic or soap to the bleeding nail. Alternate the last two steps until the bleeding has stopped.

The key is to stop the bleeding. Small bird especially are vulnerable to serious blood loss. Depending on the individual, nails need to be trimmed every three weeks or so.

Wing Clipping

To say the least, wing clipping is a controversial issue. Flying is a natural part of life for birds, and wing clipping deprives a bird of an important form of self-expression and needed exercise. On the other

If you decide to clip your bird's wings, have an experienced person show you how first.

hand, a bird flying free around the house can be a danger to himself and to valuable household objects. The best of all worlds is a large aviary for your bird to experience freer flight, but that is out of the reach of most people. Therefore, you must weigh different aspects of the bird's welfare to make a correct decision.

Larger, social birds sometimes have their wings clipped. Clipping the wings keeps the birds safer, but it also takes away the quality that makes them a bird: the ability fly. Of course ostriches can't fly, and I suppose that's a good thing.

Most vets will trim wings and can show you how to do it. If you attempt to trim the bird's wings yourself, be careful. If done correctly this procedure causes no pain to the bird. You will need a helper to hold the bird carefully. Clip only to the point that the bird can glide safely to the floor. Using very sharp wing scissors, remove the ends of the outer six or seven feathers (the flight feathers). Clip both wings symmetrically so that the bird will not be unbalanced.

Clip only mature flight feathers, which have no nerves. Immature, or blood feathers, should not be cut, as the bird will bleed profusely. Wing feathers other than flight feathers are used for protection and shouldn't be trimmed. With poor-flying birds, you can get away with trimming half to two-thirds of the feather length outside the coverts of the six end flight feathers. Better flyers need shorter trims. Trimming should be done frequently; it's amazing how fast they can grow back. Recheck the wings every month or so.

Bathing

In their native tropical environment, most birds get frequent baths. Birds enjoy bathing, and it helps them retain their natural preening habits as well. (Most contemporary houses are really too dry to be ideal for birds. Generally, birds like it humid.) Regular bathing helps keep the skin in good condition and colors vibrant. Make sure the room is sufficiently warm. You can use a regular plant mister

and plastic dish for the bird's bath; it's best if you use these items only for this purpose. Put about an inch of lukewarm water in the bottom of the dish.

There are some commercial preparations available for this purpose, but they don't really have an advantage over ordinary tap water. Some of them may even be harmful to your bird. Some bird owners even take their birds into the shower with them, and you can buy special perches just for this purpose.

Many birds enjoy being misted, but others prefer to have a bathing basin. Try both and see which your bird likes better.

Do not bathe a sick bird. Healthy individuals vary in how often they like baths; trial and error will help you and your bird arrive upon a mutually agreeable schedule.

Household Dangers

Many things we consider harmless are toxic to birds, and most things toxic to us are toxic to them, too. Some toxins include dishwasher detergent, drain cleaners, floor and furniture polish,

Dangers

Running fans, open toilets, and kitchen toxins can be deadly to birds. It's fine to let the bird loose, but please keep her safe.

gasoline and kerosene, matches, crayons, mothballs, snail bait, iodine, boric acid, nail polish, paint remover, and lye.

Lead

Lead is a toxic metal. However, it is soft and apparently fun to chew for birds. It can be found in bird toys weighted with lead (avoid them), old costume jewelry, lead caulking in stained-glass windows, fishing weights, curtain weights, and certain kinds of screens and wires. Newspaper, lead pencils, and paint manufactured within the last twenty years are safe.

Airborne Toxins

Scented candles, pot-pourri pots, incense, carpet or air fresheners, ammonia or bleach fumes, and even some perfumes can be dangerous. And don't smoke around your bird. It's bad for both of you. Teflon and similar products, if burned, emit toxic fumes (polytetra-fluoroethylene) that are deadly to your bird. No item with a nonstick coating should be kept near your bird--even when it is not being heated. In fact, birds are so sensitive, that if you can smell something, it's probably not really good for the bird.

Electricity

A bird can chew through an electrical cord in the blink of an eye, and probably will if you don't watch her. For some reason, birds are tremendously attracted to electrical cords (might be the texture). Supervision is the main key to keeping your bird out of trouble.

Physical Dangers

If your bird is flighted, cover windows with curtain so the bird doesn't go crashing into them. If the window is open, check to make sure the screen is in place and free of holes. Mirrors are also dangerous; birds don't instinctively understand them. Rooms with stuccoed ceilings can also create a hazard for your bird if she scrapes her head against them.

Plant Poisons

Plants toxic to birds include American yew (needles and seeds), avocado, baneberry (berries and roots), bird of paradise (seeds), calla lily (leaves), caladium (leaves), daphne (berries), holly (berries), Dieffenbachia or dumbcane (leaves), eggplant (all parts but the fruit), elephant's ear (leaves and stem), Japanese yew (needles and seeds), Jerusalem cherry (berries), juniper (needles, stems, berries), lobelia (all parts), mistletoe (berries), mock orange (fruit), morning glory (all parts), nightshades (berries and leaves), oleander (almost all parts), philodendron (leaves and stem), poinsettia (leaves and flowers), rhododendron (all parts), sweet pea (seeds and fruits), and wisteria (leaves and fruit).

Even temperature fluctuation is harmful to some delicate birds, and the kitchen is the room in which temperature fluctuates the most. Moderate, gradual changes (10 or 20 degrees) are usually tolerated quite well. Drafts can be especially tough on more delicate species. Cover the fireplace when not in use. In fact, even burning some kinds of wood is dangerous to birds.

Identifying Your Bird

You may be able to recognize your bird in any lineup, but to make sure everyone else does, it's important to get her ID'd. Many homegrown birds will come with a band already that is engraved with a series of letters or numbers to identify the breeder and perhaps the date of the bird's birth. Be sure you write down this information and keep it in a safe place.

Bird Health Care

Nobody wants a sick pet, but bird health can't be accepted as a given, either. Most caged birds are tropical animals transported to a strange climate and unnatural circumstances. All this is stressful. To make sure your bird stays in peak form, partner up with an avian veterinarian, who is—next to you—your bird's best friend.

Finding a Vet

Many vets simply aren't familiar with a bird's special needs. If you have a general vet for other pets, you may ask him to recommend an avian vet. If not, your best bet is to find a veterinarian certified by the American Board of Veterinary Practitioners (ABVP). These initials will follow his veterinary degree (usually DVM). This certificate means that the vet has a certain amount of clinical experience with birds. He may specialize even further, of course. Many avian vets also belong to the Association of Avian Veterinarians; however, this is just an association and requires no special competence in the field. It does usually signify that the vet in question has a particular interest in birds.

The Vet Checkup

Your bird will benefit from a twice-yearly veterinary checkup. As part of a regular exam, please allow your vet to conduct a CBC, or complete blood count. This is an important diagnostic tool that can uncover many avian diseases including anemia and parasites, dangerous problems that you may not otherwise know about until it is too late. Other common diagnostic tests include electrophoresis (EPH, SPE) for the immune system and the AST (also called SGOT) assay to check for liver and muscle damage.

Taking Your Bird to the Vet

If you take your bird to vet, bring with you all the information your vet can use to help him diagnose the problem. This will include a fresh sample of the droppings (unpleasant, but important). If you suspect your bird has eaten something toxic, bring a sample of that as well, or the container it came from. If your bird is already on a prescription medication, be sure to have all that information at hand.

Carry Along

In order to make the trip to the vet, consider getting a traveling cage. You can also use a small animal carrier with a perch installed. Using treats, you can train your bird to go in the carrier without a struggle.

Some birds suddenly seem to recover themselves once at the vets. This doesn't mean she is well. It means she's alert to danger and possibly trying to hide any signs of illness. In the wild, a sick bird is a dead bird. Don't be fooled by this primitive tactic.

While at the vet's, don't be afraid to ask questions. Here are some of my favorites:

Taking your bird to the vet will be much easier if you train your bird to get into a carrier or traveling cage voluntarily.

- "What does my bird have?"
- "What's the prognosis?"
- "Is the disease curable?"
- "If not, will it eventually kill your bird?"
- "What's the best course of action and how will it help my bird?"
- "How will this disease and its treatment affect my bird?"
- "What responsibility will I have in her care?"
- "How much will this cost?"
- "Should my bird see an avian specialist?"

Medicating Your Bird

Sadly, birds just aren't very cooperative about taking medicine. Luckily, most bird medications are liquids with a pleasant flavor that you can administer by eyedropper. To give the bird the drug, wrap her in a towel, carefully including her feet and wings. Place the tip of the syringe just inside the beak and slowly drop it in. Let the bird swallow.

In some cases, you'll notice some liquid coming from the bird's nostrils. This usually isn't dangerous, but stop giving the medication, let the bird relax, and check with your vet. After giving the medicine, reward your bird with a treat for being so good.

Typical Signs of Illness

Most birds remain healthy for most of their lives, but like the rest of creation, they are prone to certain illnesses. Your careful observation and quick follow-up can help keep most diseases in check.

While every disease has different signs, the following are danger signals: diarrhea, depression, lethargy, extended periods in the bottom of the cage, fluffed-up appearance, inattention to grooming/poor appearance, irritability, less vocalizing or a change in voice quality, loss of appetite, matted feathers, runny nostrils, scaling or crusting of skin, shut eyes, and unusual breathing pattern.

Common Ailments

Aspergillosis

This respiratory disease is caused by the fungus *Aspergillus*, which is found in warm, humid environments, especially in dusty, poorly ventilated areas. Healthy birds can usually fight off the fungus, but

If your bird's feathers are constantly ruffled or fluffed up, she may be ill. Seek veterinary attention promptly because birds can go downhill rapidly.

Giving the Meds

In a few cases, you can add the medicine directly to the bird's drinking water. Ask your vet if this is acceptable in your bird's case.

stressed or weak birds are potential targets. Parrots and mynah birds are the most common victims.

Birds with the acute form of the disease typically have difficulty in breathing and turn rather blue. This may result in sudden death. More common is chronic aspergillosis, but it too can be deadly. Signs include respiratory problems, trouble vocalizing, and discharges from the nares (nostrils). If the disease is caught in time, surgery can remove some lesions caused by the fungus, and antifungal drugs may be administered. However, this is a very serious condition, and a cure is not guaranteed.

Cnemidocoptes Mites

Also known as scaly face and scaly leg mites, this condition is characterized by a buildup of scales on the feet or beak, causing deformities of the latter. Parakeets are most susceptible, but canaries can get it as well. You may notice white crusty lesions on non-feathered skin. In parakeets, lesions usually begin at the corners of the beak and have a honeycombed appearance. Foot lesions are common in canaries. Consult your vet for proper treatment.

Bleeding Feathers

A bleeding feather is almost certainly a pinfeather, one that is young and still growing. It usually occurs on the wing. You should remove the bleeding feather to stop the bleeding. Simply take some tweezers or forceps as high above the crack as possible and pluck it from the follicle, firmly but gently. Hold the bone of the wing with the other hand. If the follicle continues to bleed, press on it firmly, but do not apply a clotting agent. Let your bird rest in a dark, quiet room afterwards. If bleeding continues, take your bird to the vet.

Egg Binding

This condition is extremely serious, even leading to death. The condition can occur in any bird but is quite common in smaller species like parakeets, finches, canaries, cockatiels, and lovebirds. Causes can include poor nutrition, overproduction of eggs, obesity, infections, old age, stress, and lack of exercise. Birds who are strongly attached to their owners seem particularly affected. Signs include depression, a wide-legged stance, straining, loss of appetite, distended abdomen, and shaking of the tail. If your bird exhibits any of these signs, she should see an avian vet right away. Small birds can die within hours if untreated.

Feather Picking

Feather picking is really more a behavior than a disease, but since disease may be at the root of it, I will include it here. Physical causes are legion: allergies, infection, metabolic or endocrine disease, poor

nutrition, drug reactions, toxins, bad wing trims, broken blood feather, tumors, and environmental conditions, such as low humidity, lack of natural sunlight, and overcrowding. Inducers include boredom and frustration.

Feather picking is often a behavioral problem caused by boredom or stress, but it can be caused by parasites, allergies, or other medical conditions.

To cure the problem, you'll need to identify the cause, which may require a trip to the avian vet for a workup that includes a physical exam and lab tests. Once the underlying condition is addressed, the feather plucking should stop.

Can You Get Sick from Your Bird?

Birds carry several zoonotic diseases (the fancy term for diseases people and animals can give to each other). It is unlikely that this will actually happen, but chronically ill people, elderly people, and people who are immune-compromised can be at risk.

Canary Poxvirus

This viral disease primarily affects canaries kept outside who ingest or inhale the virus. Mosquitoes also can transmit the disease. Signs include fluffed feathers, loss of appetite, and lethargy. Victims develop pneumonia, and many die within two to three days. Other kinds of poxviruses affect other species. There is no specific treatment, but supportive care may sometimes help pull a bird through.

Psittacine Beak and Feather Disease (PBFD)

This is a highly contagious condition that deforms flight and tail feathers, as well as causing beak deformities and eventually death in many individuals. Survivors of the disease appear to be "vaccinated" against a further occurrence. It often appears along with the polyoma virus, and has both acute and chronic forms. Affected birds are sometimes called "creepers" for the obvious reason that they cannot fly. It was first noted in the 1970s in cockatoos and has since been observed in more than 40 species of birds. While the virus can be detected in the bird's blood a couple of days after it becomes infected, the characteristic wing and beak troubles don't start until perhaps two months after. This disease is particularly common in cockatoos. Most affected birds are under two years of age. There is no specific treatment, unfortunately. The only thing the owner can do is provide good supportive therapy. Sadly, this is a progressive condition from which few birds recover; most die within two years.

Psittacosis (Parrot fever or Chlamydiosis)

This condition is caused by the bacterium *Chlamydia psittaci*. This disease can be transmitted to people, especially older folks. Some species, notably the cockatiel, tend to be carriers only and show no clinical signs of the disease. The disease is transmitted through infected feces and also through the air. Affected birds usually become depressed, and may have diarrhea or problems breathing. If left untreated, most succumb, but it can be treated with the antibiotic doxycycline.

Vitamin A Deficiency

This is a condition found in birds fed only seed. Such birds often show tiny white patches in the mouth and tongue. These are very painful and can enlarge to the point where the bird has trouble swallowing or even breathing. If you seen any sign that this is happening, consult your vet and begin vitamin A supplementation right away. Of course, the disease is best prevented by using a formulated food as well as feeding your bird dark leafy green vegetables that are rich in this vitamin. Apples, bananas, oranges, lettuce, and corn are low in vitamin A. Broccoli, sweet potatoes, carrots, squash, and peaches have high amounts.

Vomiting and Regurgitation

This behavior is not a disease itself, but a sign of another condition, including bacterial, fungal, viral, or parasitic infection. Heart, liver, or kidney disease, as well as diabetes, may also produce vomiting. Other conditions like electrolyte imbalance, toxin ingestion, and poor nutrition may also be responsible. See your vet as soon as possible.

Yeast Infections (Candidiasis)

While this yeast occurs in low numbers in the normal digestive tract, if it overgrows it can cause problems to the digestive and repository system, as well as affecting the beak. Some birds (primarily finches or canaries) may also get skin infections from the yeast. Signs include white growths on the beak or in the mouth and

Sneezing

An occasional sneeze is nothing to worry about, but frequent sneezing, especially when accompanied by other signs of illness, such as nasal discharge, can be serious. Causes might include bacterial or fungal infection, poor nutrition, and foreign bodies in the nasal passage. Talk to your vet.

bad breath. It is very common in young cockatiels. Treatment includes the administration of antifungal medications.

Bird First Aid

While an avian veterinarian is your best resource when it comes to dealing with your bird's health, in an emergency, there are some steps your can take.

Wounds and Bleeding

First identify the source of the bleeding. If it's from a feather, remove it. Do not use a styptic powder in the follicle. Clean the area with a liquid antiseptic like povidone-iodine or chlorhexidine. Don't use a cream, which can harm the feathers and close in the wound.

If the tongue, beak, or nail is lacerated (a frequent accident) mix a solution of cold water and powdered alum; dip the wounded part in the solution repeatedly until the bleeding stops. Seek veterinary attention if bleeding persists for long.

Concussion

If your bird flies into the wall, and seems stunned, put her in a quiet, warm, dark room. Call your vet if she does not return to normal behavior quickly.

Protruding Tissue

If you notice any tissue extruding from your bird's vent area, keep the tissue moist with petroleum jelly and call your vet.

Your Avian First-Aid Kit

Here are some basic items you can use to help your bird in an emergency or to get through an illness. Keep the material together in a large, labeled box. Write the name and phone number of your vet on the top.

- Eyedropper
- Eye irrigation solution
- Gauze bandages and cotton balls
- Hand-feeding formula
- Heating pad
- Electrolyte solution
- Nail clippers and file
- Scissors
- Styptic powder
- Tweezers

Poison

If your bird gets a noxious substance in her eyes, wash them with lukewarm water. If there are fumes, remove the bird from the area and ventilate the place. If she has eaten something, call your vet immediately.

By knowing the signs of bird diseases and possible associated conditions, and by having a good relationship with your vet, you and your bird should enjoy a long and happy companionship. Happy birding.

Resources

ORGANIZATIONS

American Federation of Aviculture
P.O. Box 7312
N. Kansas City, MO 64116
Telephone: (816) 421-2473
Fax: (816) 421-3214
E-mail: afaoffice@aol.com
http://www.afabirds.org/

Aviculture Society of the United Kingdom
Arcadia-The Mounts-East Allington-Totnes
Devon TQ9 7QJ
United Kingdom
E-mail: admin@avisoc.co.uk
http://www.avisoc.co.uk/

PUBLICATIONS

Bird Talk **Magazine**
3 Burroughs
Irvine, CA 92618
Telephone: (949) 855-8822
Fax: (949) 855-3045
http://www.birdtalkmagazine.com/bt/

Bird Times **Magazine**
7-L Dundas Circle
Greensboro, NC 27407
Telephone: (336) 292-4047
Fax: (336) 292-4272
E-mail: info@petpublishing.com
www.birdtimes.com

Good Bird **Magazine**
PO Box 684394
Austin, TX 78768
Telephone: (512) 423-7734
Fax: (512) 236-0531
Email: info@goodbirdinc.com
http: //www.GoodBirdInc.com

INTERNET RESOURCES

Bird CLICK
(www.geocities.com/Heartland/Acres/9154)
A site and e-mail list devoted to clicker
training pet birds.

Exotic Pet Vet. Net
(http://www.exoticpetvet.net)
This website, authored by an avian veterinarian and an aviculturist/zoologist, offers
extensive information on a variety of bird-
related topics, including nutrition, health,
and emergency care.

VETERINARY RESOURCES

Association of Avian Veterinarians (AAV)
P.O. Box 811720
Boca Raton, FL 33481-1720
Telephone: (561) 393-8901
Fax: (561) 393-8902
E-mail: AAVCTRLOFC@aol.com
http://www.aav.org/

EMERGENCY RESOURCES AND RES-
CUE ORGANIZATIONS

ASPCA Animal Poison Control Center
Telephone: (888) 426-4435
E-mail: napcc@aspca.org (for non-emer-
gency, general information only)
http://www.apcc.aspca.org

Bird Hotline
P.O. Box 1411
Sedona, AZ 86339-1411
E-mail: birdhotline@birdhotline.com
http://www.birdhotline.com/

Bird Placement Program
P.O. Box 347392
Parma, OH 44134
Telephone: (330) 722-1627
E-mail: birdrescue5@hotmail.com
www.birdrescue.com

The Gabriel Foundation
1025 Acoma Street
Denver, CO 80204
http://www.thegabrielfoundation.org
A nonprofit corporation promoting educa-
tion, conservation, rescue, rehabilitation,
adoption, and sanctuary for the needs of
parrots everywhere.

Index

Photo Credits: